DENES AGAY'S
LEARNING TO PLAY PIANO
BOOK 1: PRIMER

A progression of melodic pieces and
studies teaching the basics step by step.

Nancy Bachus, Associate Editor

Book design by Margo Dittmer
Interior illustrations by Janice Fried

Copyright © 1987, 1991 by Yorktown Music Press, Inc.
All Rights Reserved.

Order No. YK 20485
US International Standard Book Number: 0.8256.8069.7
UK International Standard Book Number: 0.7119.1014.6

Exclusive Distributors:
Music Sales Corporation
257 Park Avenue South, New York, NY 10010 USA
Music Sales Limited
8/9 Frith Street, London W1V 5TZ England
Music Sales Pty. Limited
120 Rothschild Street, Rosebery, Sydney, NSW 2018, Australia

Printed in the United States of America by
Vicks Lithograph and Printing Corporation

Yorktown Music Press, Inc.
New York/London/Sydney

New Revised Edition with Color Guide

CONTENTS

POSITION AT THE PIANO

⭐ Sit with a straight back facing the middle of the keyboard—leaning very slightly forward.

⭐ Feet should be on the floor. A footstool or box can be used if feet do not reach the floor.

⭐ Allow the upper arm to hang loosely. Adjust seat so that elbow, wrist, and hand are at the height of the keyboard.

Hand Position

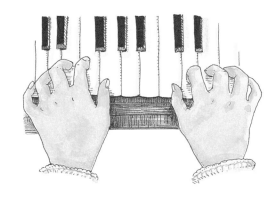

⭐ Hands are cupped with palms down as if holding a small, round object like a ball.

⭐ Fingers are curved, with the fleshy part, not the nails, touching the keys.

Finger Numbers

⭐ When playing the piano our fingers have numbers. The thumb is the first finger in each hand.

⭐ Practice the finger numbers this way: Hold your hands in front of you as shown above, fingers spread, and wiggle each finger as its number is called out by your teacher. At first, practice this separately with each hand, then with the two hands together.

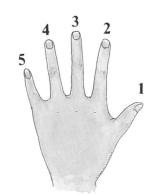
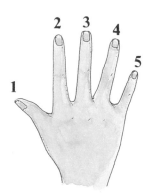

See also *The Technic Companion*, pp. 6–8 "Natural Hand Position."

THE KEYBOARD

The piano has white keys and black keys. The white keys are in a row touching each other.
The black keys are raised and arranged in groups of twos and threes.

⭐ Draw a circle around all groups of two black keys on this keyboard:

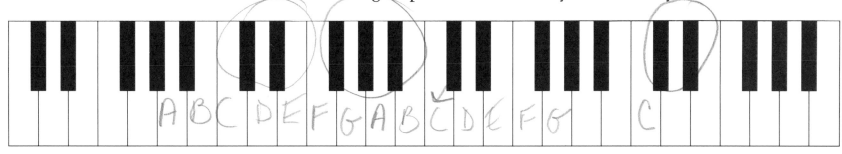

⭐ Make a loose fist—raise your hand and "fall" on the group of two black keys with a loose wrist. (Do this with each hand individually.)

⭐ Put the middle (3rd) fingers of both hands on neighboring black keys in the "two-black-key" group. Play and sing this little song. (Your teacher will show you how.)

⭐ Place the middle (third) finger of your left hand on a black key in the "three-black-key" group and play a melody of your own invention to fit these words. (Sing the words as you play.)

"Three black keys, Three black keys, I can play on three black keys"

⭐ Now place the middle finger of your right hand on one of the three black keys and play another melody to fit the same words.

See also *The Technic Companion*, pp. 9–11.

DIRECTIONS ON THE KEYBOARD

Each key, white or black, produces a different tone.

Going to the *left,* or going *down* the keyboard, tones become gradually *lower.*

Going to the *right,* or going *up* the keyboard, tones become gradually *higher.*

Lower tones to the left

Higher tones to the right

down

up

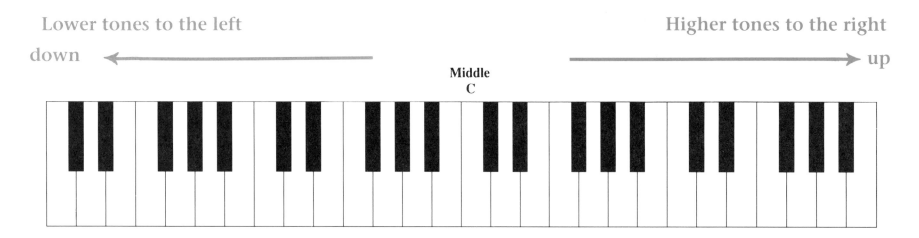

★ Place the middle (3rd) finger of your right hand on Middle C and play eight white keys, going higher step-by-step. Sing the words.

★ Repeat with the left hand, playing down from Middle C, singing the words.

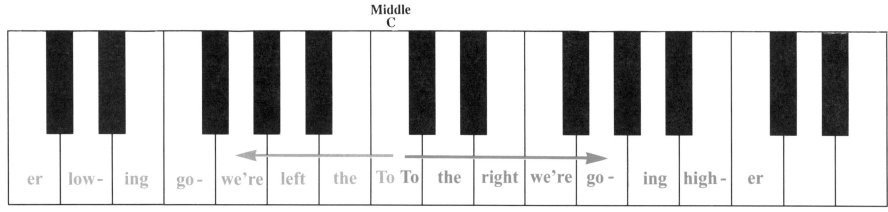

Left Hand
(plays after right hand)

Right Hand
(plays first)

PLAYING BY FINGER NUMBERS
with the three middle fingers (2-3-4)

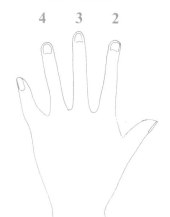

Left Hand

4 3 2

☆ Put your two hands on the keyboard in this position.

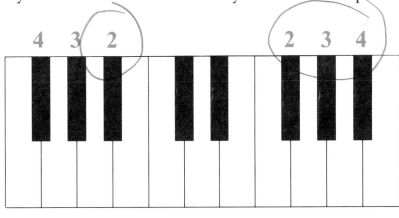

4 3 2   2 3 4

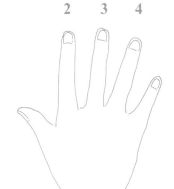

Right Hand

2 3 4

Merrily We Roll Along

☆ Play and sing:

Observe that the finger numbers follow the rise and fall of the melody.
Words underlined are held twice as long as the other words.
(Such combinations of long and short tones give music its patterns of rhythm.)

L.H.   2   2   2   2   2   2   2

       3   3   3   3   3

       4

Mer - ri - ly   we   roll   a - <u>long</u> ,   roll   a - <u>long</u> ,   roll   a - <u>long</u> ,

R.H.   4   4   4   4   4

       3   3   3   3   3

       2   2

Mer - ri - ly   we   roll   a - <u>long</u> ,   O'er   the   deep   blue   <u>sea</u> .

See also *The Technic Companion*, pp. 13–14.

MORE PLAYING BY FINGER NUMBERS
with all five fingers

Place your hands on the keyboard as shown on this chart.

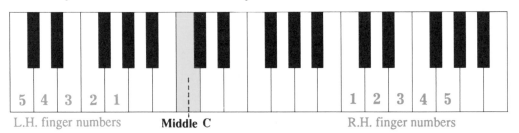

L.H. finger numbers   **Middle C**   R.H. finger numbers

With each hand separately, using all fingers as shown by the finger numbers,
1. First, play "in the air."
2. Then, tap on the fallboard or keys.

3. Finally, play these melodies, stepping from one white key to its neighbor and calling out the finger numbers.
4. Always, press down the keys gently but firmly; fingers should maintain their curved position.

Here is another melody you can play by the finger numbers.

Here We Go

Use the same position on the keyboard as above.
(Underlined words are held twice as long as the others.)

1. Sing out the numbers as you play.
2. Sing the words.

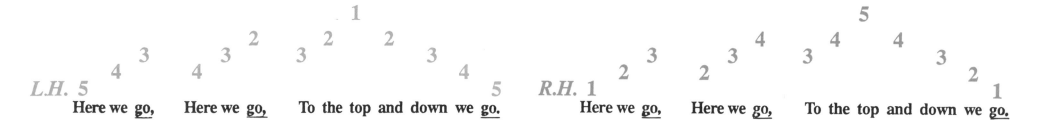

SHORT AND LONG NOTES
Note Values

★ Sing "Here We Go" again and this time, instead of playing, clap your hands as you sing.

sing:	Here	we	**go,**		Here	we	**go,**		to	the	top	and	down	we	**go.**	
clap:	x	x	x	x	x	x	x	x	x	x	x	x	x	x	x	x

Did you notice that every time you sang the word "go" you clapped your hands twice, while singing the other words you clapped only once? This means that the note sung to the word "go" is held twice as long as the notes sung to the other words; it receives two counts while the other words receive one count.

♩ This is a one-count note and is called a quarter note.

♩ This is a two-count note and is called a half note.

𝅝 This is a four-count note and is called a whole note.

To make reading notes easier, we divide music into measures with bar lines.
There is a double bar line at the end of the piece.
Sing the following melody and clap your hands in rhythm to every beat.

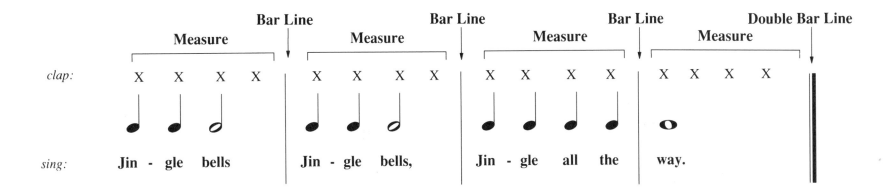

THE MUSICAL ALPHABET

The white keys of the piano are named after the first seven letters of the alphabet: **A B C D E F G**

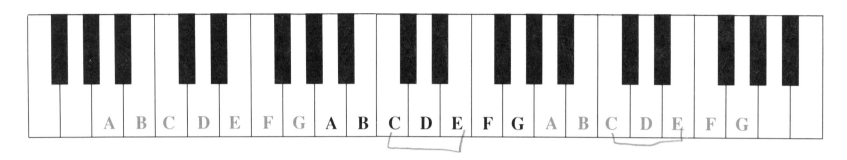

Observe that after G the letter names start again with A. (A is the white key to the left of the third black key.)

⭐ You already know the location of the Middle C. Now play all C's (to the left of the two black keys) from the lowest to the highest. How many C's are on your keyboard? _____

⭐ Play all D's from the highest to the lowest. How many D's are there? _____

⭐ Similarly locate and play all E's (to the right of the two black keys);
F's (to the left of the three black keys);
B's (to the right of the three black keys);
G's (between the first and second of the three black keys);
and A's (between the second and third of the three black keys).

⭐ Play these keys all over the keyboard. (Call out the letter names of the keys as you play.)

A B - B A 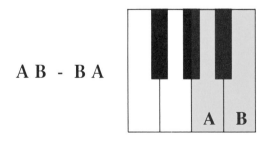   C D E - E D C    F G - G F

See also *The Technic Companion*, p. 15: "Jumping Octaves."

★ Write the letter names on the keys marked x.
   Play them (with any finger) as you call out
   the letter names.

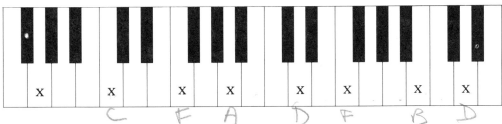

C   F   A   D   F   B   D

PLAYING BY LETTER NAMES AND FINGER NUMBERS

★ Place the first finger of the right hand on Middle C and play this melody, calling out the letter names.

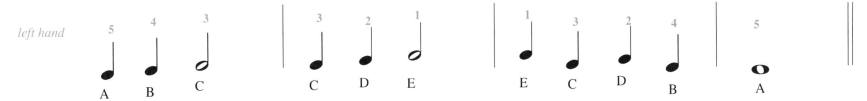

★ Place the fifth finger of the left hand on A below Middle C and play this melody as you call out the letter names.

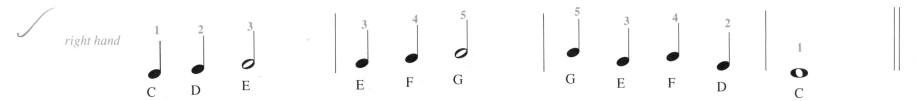

★ Play this melody. Do you recognize the tune?

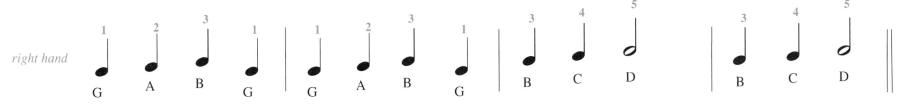

★ With the third finger of either hand play those keys whose letter names are called out by your teacher, one by one.

THE STAFF

You have seen that the notes follow the rise and fall of the melody. In order to see exactly how high or low a note is, we need some guidelines. These guidelines are called the staff, a system of five lines and four spaces, numbered from the bottom up.

Five lines   **Four spaces**

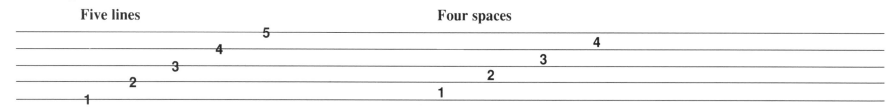

Notes on the staff are placed both on lines and in spaces.

Line Notes   Space Notes   Write four line notes.   Write four space notes.

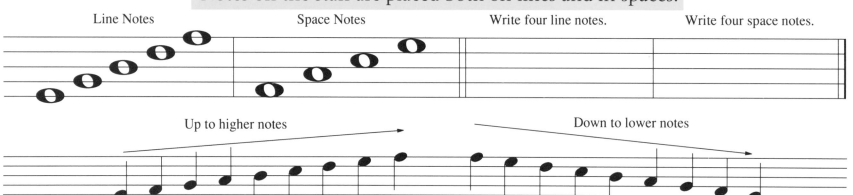

Up to higher notes   Down to lower notes

Notes on the staff may move by

Steps	**Skips**	**Repetition**
from line to next space, or from space to next line.	with one line or one space between the two notes.	stays on the same line or in the same space.

Play neighbor white keys with neighbor fingers.

Skip one white key and skip a finger.

Played on the same key using the same finger.

12

THE GRAND STAFF

For piano music two staves are used: the treble staff and the bass staff.

Trace over clef signs   Write three clefs

The **treble staff**, headed by the **treble clef**, is for higher notes, usually played by the right hand.

The **bass staff**, headed by the **bass clef**, is for lower notes, usually played by the left hand. (Observe the dots above and below the fourth line.)

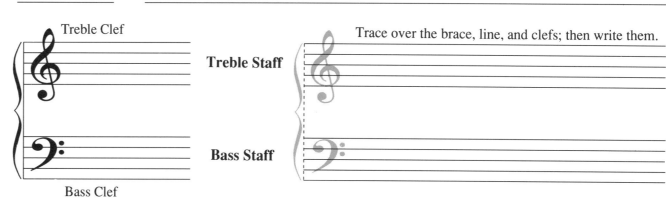

The two staves, connected by a line and a **brace** (ǀ) are called the **grand staff**.

Trace over the brace, line, and clefs; then write them.

You have seen that music is divided by bar lines into measures. Bar lines are drawn on the grand staff too. Usually each measure has the same number of beats (counts), as indicated by the time signature.

TIME SIGNATURE

2 The upper number (in this case **2**) tells us how many counts there are in a measure (two).

4 The lower number (**4**) shows what kind of note receives one count (quarter note).

Whenever the lower number is **4** in a time signature, a quarter note receives one count. 

MIDDLE C ON THE STAFF

Middle C is on a line of its own between the two staves.

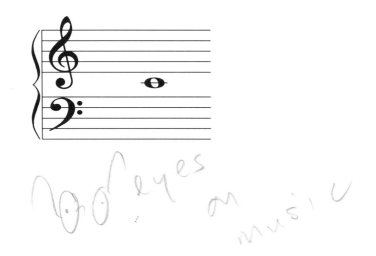

When played by the right hand, Middle C is written closer to the treble staff just below the first line.

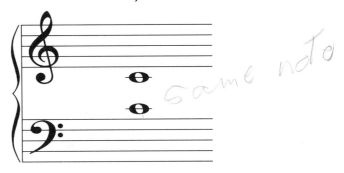

When played by the left hand, Middle C is written closer to the bass staff just above the fifth line.

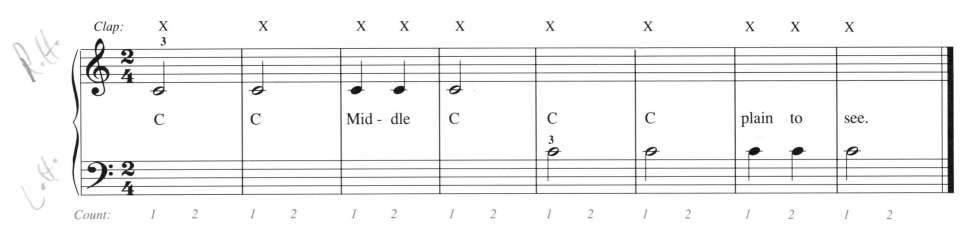

Clap: X   X   X   X   X   X   X   X   X   X

C   C   Mid - dle   C   C   C   plain   to   see.

Count: 1 2   1 2   1 2   1 2   1 2   1 2   1 2   1 2

Practice Directions:

1. Clap your hands for every note, counting aloud the proper number of beats in each measure.
2. Play the notes and call out the letter names.
3. Play the notes and count aloud the beats in each measure.
4. Play the notes and sing the words.

Skill Builder: Try playing other C's with your third finger.

14

NOTES AROUND MIDDLE C

In every piece:

☆ First, play and sing the letter names.
☆ Then play and count.

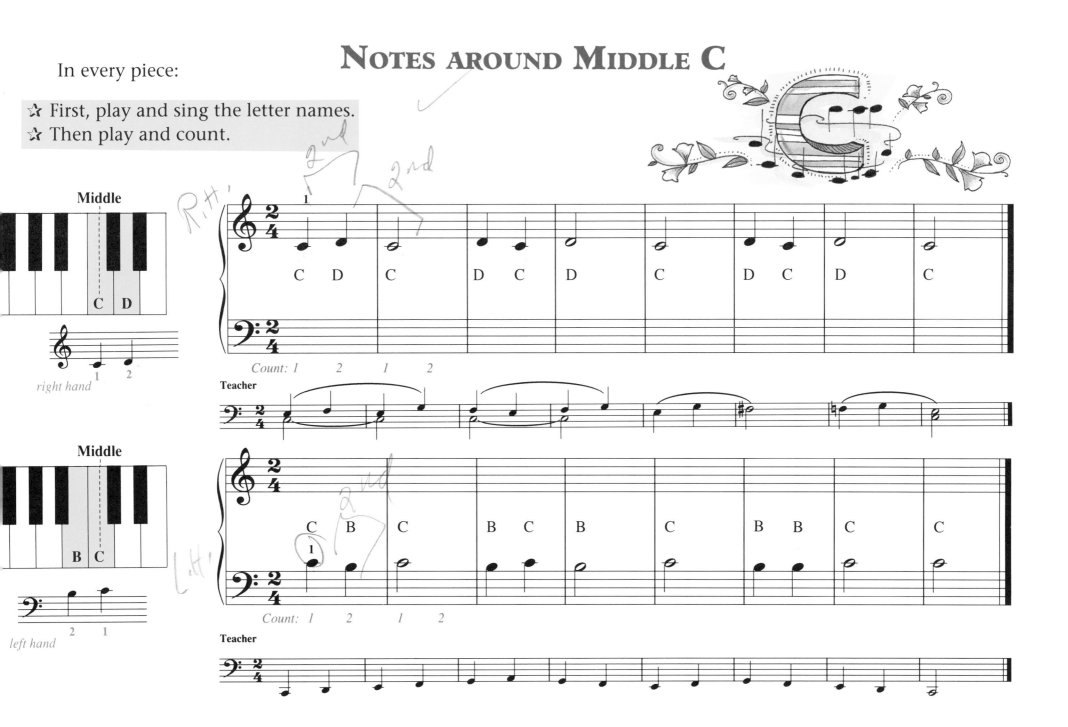

Skill Builder: Play also with fingers 2-3-2 and 3-4-3. (Play with firm nail joints.)
Play in other octaves.
Play other B's and D's all over the keyboard.

15

Three-Note Jig

Three note jig, three note jig, It's the start of some-thing big, What a joy-ful whirl-i-gig.

Teacher

True or False?
Write your answers on the lines provided.

_____ 1. Going to the right on the keyboard, tones become higher.

_____ 2. ♩ This is a quarter note which receives one count.

_____ 3. A half note (♩) receives two counts.

_____ 4. The white key between the two black keys is E.

_____ 5. The keys B and C are a step apart.

_____ 6. The time signature $\frac{2}{4}$ means that there are four counts in each measure.

INTERVALS

The distance between two notes or two keys is called an interval.
Intervals are measured and named according to the number of notes or keys involved.
In measuring intervals we count all the notes: the two notes of the interval *and* the notes (white keys) between the two.

The 2nd (Second): like a *step*

On the keyboard
A 2nd is the distance from one white key to the next white key, up or down.

On the staff
A 2nd is the distance from a line to the next space; or from a space to the next line.

☆ Play 2nds all over the keyboard with fingers 2-3, or 3-4.

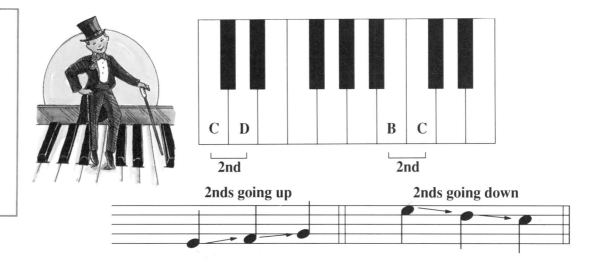

The 3rd (Third): like a *skip*

On the keyboard
A 3rd is the distance between two white keys with one white key in between them.

On the staff
A 3rd is the distance from a line to the next line, or from a space to the next space.

☆ Play 3rds all over the keyboard with fingers 1-3, 2-4, and 3-5.

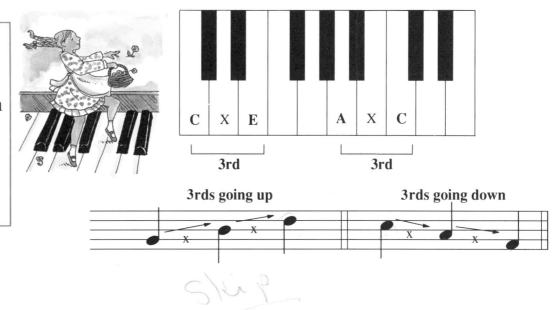

Skill Builder: Close your eyes and play 2nds and 3rds with different finger combinations.

New Time Signature

4 four counts to a measure

4 quarter note (♩) gets one count

New note: E on the first line of the treble staff (a skip above Middle C).

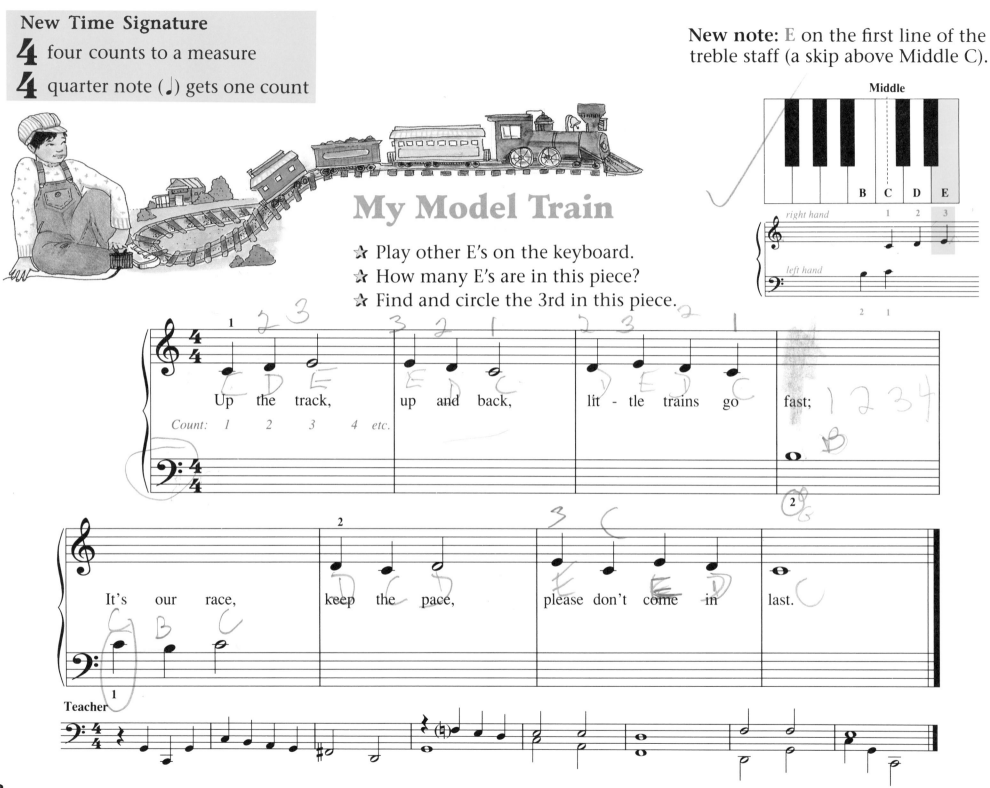

My Model Train

☆ Play other E's on the keyboard.

☆ How many E's are in this piece?

☆ Find and circle the 3rd in this piece.

Up the track, up and back, lit - tle trains go fast;

Count: 1 2 3 4 etc.

It's our race, keep the pace, please don't come in last.

Teacher

The Willow Tree

★ How many 3rds (skips) are in this piece?
★ How many 2nds (steps)?

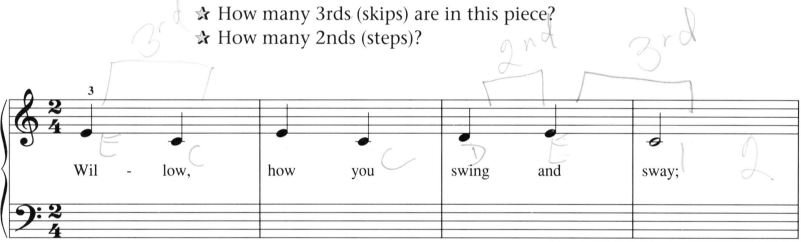

Wil - low, how you swing and sway;

Un - der you I love to play.

Teacher

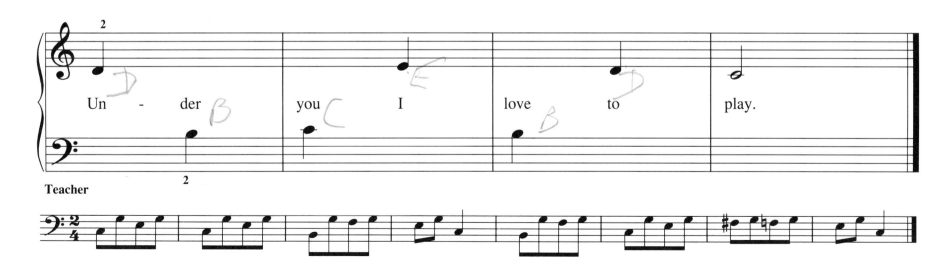

Play every piece at least three times:
1. Play and sing the letter names.
2. Play and count the beats.
3. Play and sing the words.
(Always *listen* for beautiful tone.)

New note: **A** on the fifth line of the bass staff (a skip below Middle C).

Rain, Go Away

☆ Play A's throughout the keyboard.
☆ How many A's are in this piece?

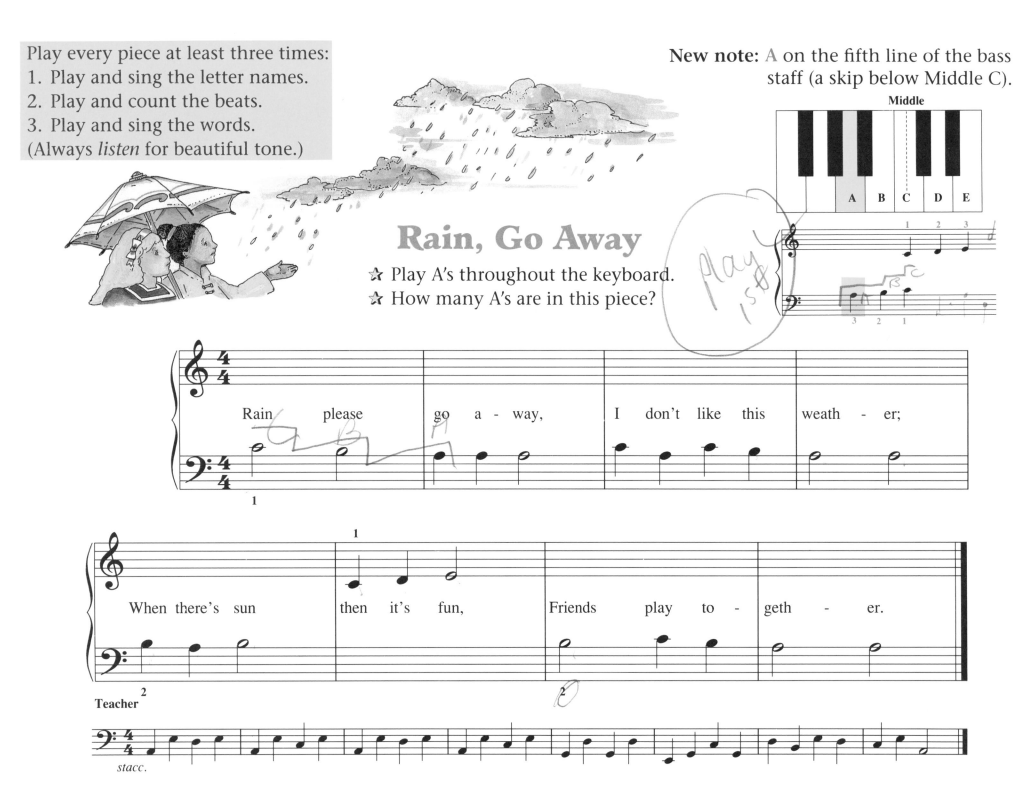

Rain   please   go   a - way,   I   don't   like   this   weath - er;

When there's sun   then   it's   fun,   Friends   play   to - geth - er.

Teacher

stacc.

20

The A-C-E Song

☆ Point out all 3rds to your teacher.

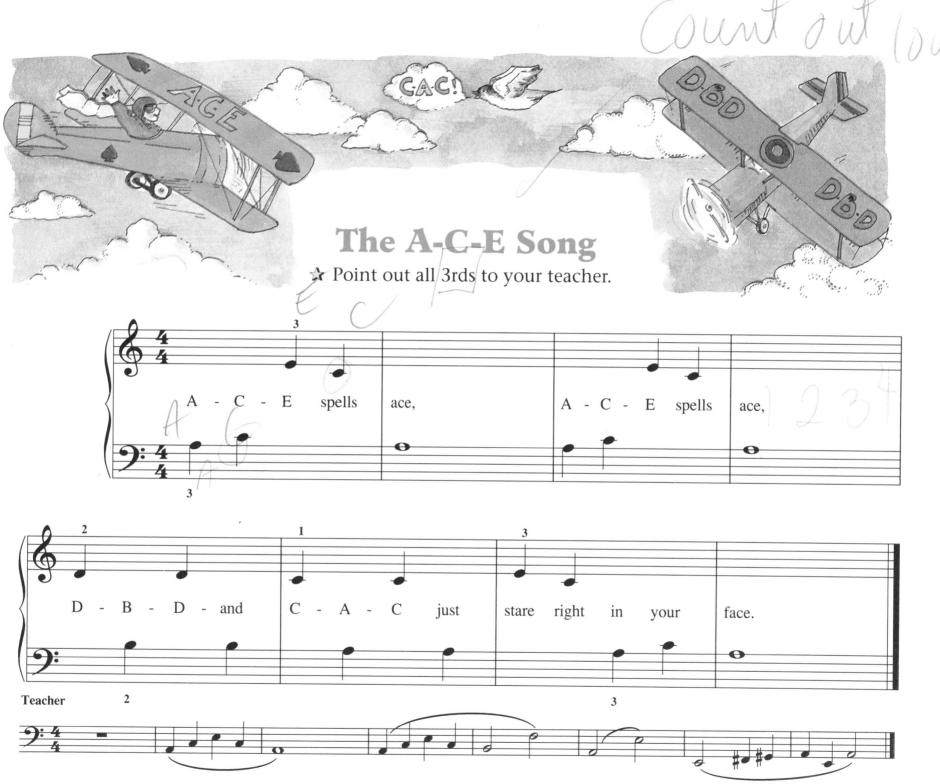

A - C - E spells ace, A - C - E spells ace,

D - B - D - and C - A - C just stare right in your face.

Teacher

NEW NOTE VALUE

𝅗𝅥. = dotted half note
(three counts)

count: 1 2 3   1 2 3   1 2 3

New Time Signature
3 three counts to a measure
4 quarter note (♩) gets one count

First Serenade

Lis - ten, I'll sing you my first ser - e - nade; You can sing with me each time that it's played.

Learn ev - 'ry word, then sing like a bird, Best ser - e - nade that you ev - er have heard.

Teacher

p = *piano* = soft
f = *forte* = loud

Reluctant Sleepy Head

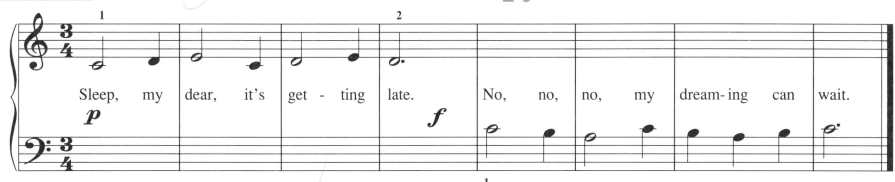

Sleep, my dear, it's get - ting late. No, no, no, my dream-ing can wait.

p

f

Repeat this piece playing the right-hand part an octave (eight keys) higher, and the left-hand part an octave lower.

The Evening Bell

Optional teacher-student duet:
1. Student plays only bass or treble part.
2. Student may use both hands, playing octaves.
3. Vary dynamics and tone quality.

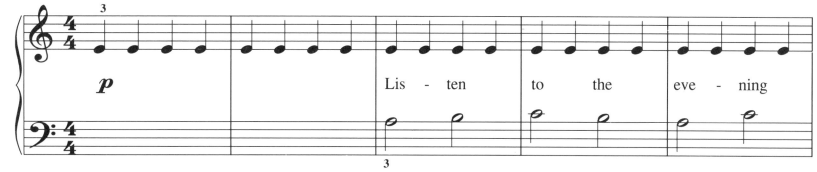

p

Lis - ten to the eve - ning

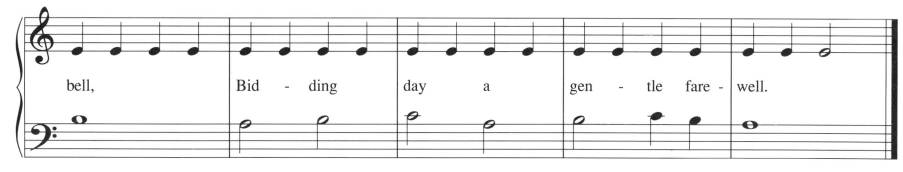

bell, Bid - ding day a gen - tle fare - well.

23

☆ Play G's (and then F's) throughout the keyboard.
Move in an arc ⌒ when jumping octaves.

New notes: F in the first space of the treble staff
G in the fourth space of the bass staff

Our Flag

There is no	love - li - er	sight in the	world,

Look at our flag as it waves when un - furled!

See also *The Technic Companion*, p. 16.

24

Yankee Doodle

New Interval: The 4th

On the keyboard
A **4th** is the distance between two white keys with two keys in between them (xx).

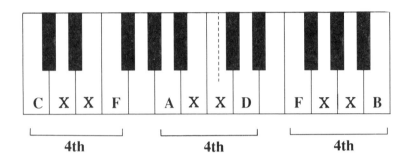

On the staff
A **4th** is the distance from a line to a space, or from a space to a line, with a line and a space skipped.

4th going up   **4th going down**

☆ Play 4ths, up and down, all over the keyboard with fingers 1-4 and 2-5.

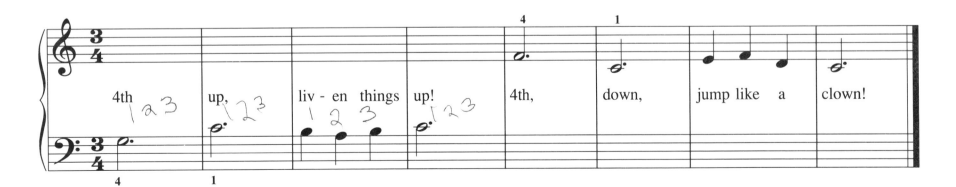

4th _1 2 3_ up, _1 2 3_ liv - en things _1 2 3_ up! _1 2 3_ 4th, down, jump like a clown!

OCTAVE SIGN

The symbol *8va* and a dotted line over the notes (*8va - - - -*) mean that you play these notes an octave (eight keys) *higher*.
The same sign under the notes means that you play these notes an octave *lower*.

Polka Time

★ Circle all 4ths in this piece.
★ How many 3rds are there?
★ How many 2nds?

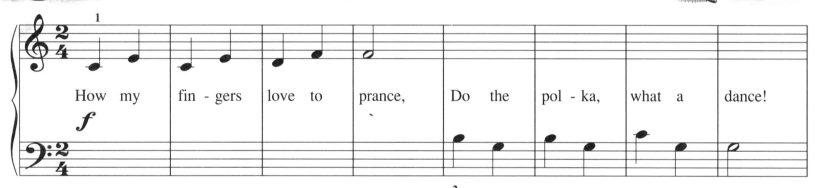

How my fin - gers love to prance, Do the pol - ka, what a dance!

Way up high it still sounds fine, Down an oc - tave it's di - vine.

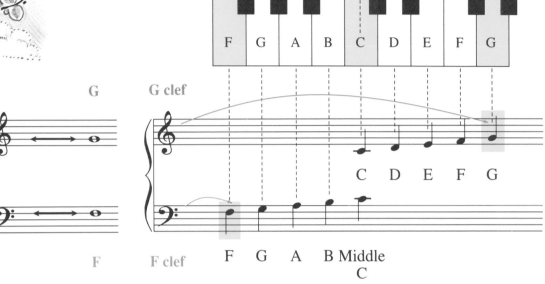

The **treble clef** is also called the **G clef** because its graceful design curls around the second line of the treble staff where the G above Middle C is located.

The **bass clef** is also called the **F Clef** because its design originates on the fourth line of the bass staff where F below Middle C is located. (Notice that the two dots of the F clef surround the F line.)

WARM-UP IN $\frac{6}{4}$ TIME

6 six counts to a measure
4 quarter-note gets one count

☆ Circle all F's and G's.
☆ Play this piece and call out the letter names of the notes.
☆ Then play it again and count aloud the beats in each measure.
☆ Then play it and sing the words.

Count: 1 2 3 4 5 6

See how high we go,   Play-ing in a row.   Let's go jump-ing now,   I will show you how.

See also *The Technic Companion*, p. 17.

Snowflakes

Use the same hand position as you did on page 28.

☆ Play this piece four ways:

1. Play as written.
2. Play the left-hand part as written and the right-hand part an octave higher.
3. Play the right-hand part as written and the left-hand part an octave lower.
4. Play the right-hand part an octave higher and the left-hand part an octave lower.

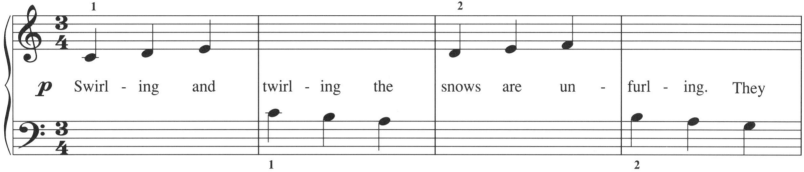

p Swirl - ing and twirl - ing the snows are un - furl - ing. They

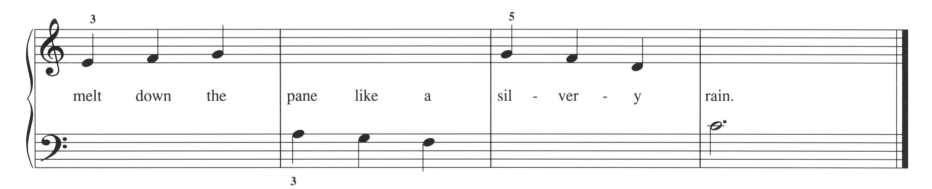

melt down the pane like a sil - ver - y rain.

I'm Waltzing!

Use the same hand position as you did on page 28.

Technic hint: When the two hands play together, each one playing a different note, make sure that the finger of the left hand and the finger of the right hand strike the keys exactly together.

★ Circle all 4ths.

See also *The Technic Companion*, p. 19.

NEW INTERVAL: THE 5TH

On the keyboard
A **5th** is the distance between two white keys with three white keys in between them (xxx).

On the staff
A **5th** is the distance from a line to a line, or from a space to a space, with one line and two spaces, or one space and two lines, skipped.

☆ Play 5ths, up and down, all over the keyboard with fingers 1-5.

left hand

5th   up,   5th   down,   There's   no   need   to   frown.

right hand

5th   down,   5th   up,   Things   are   look - ing   up!

Hop Scotch

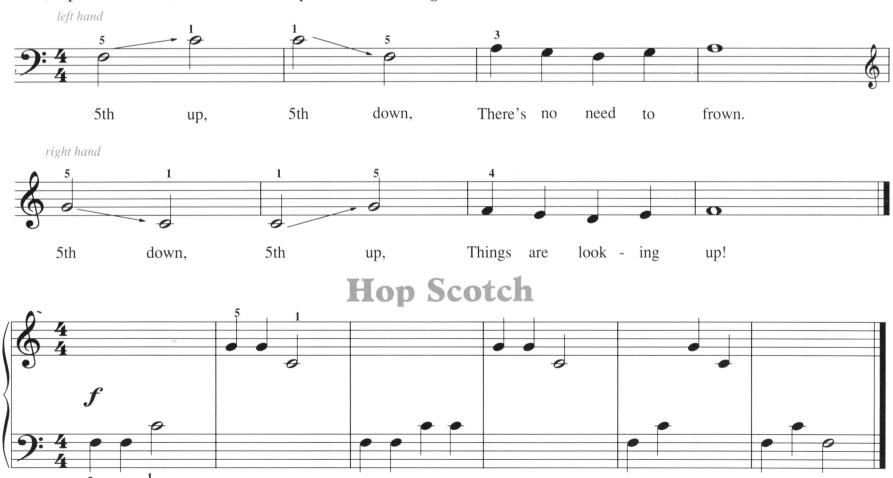

Rest signs indicate periods of silence in music.

This sign, a little beam hanging from the fourth line, is called a **whole rest**. It indicates silence in one whole measure of any kind.

Early Morning

Use the same hand position as you did on page 28.

☆ Circle the 5ths in this piece.
☆ How many 3rds are there?

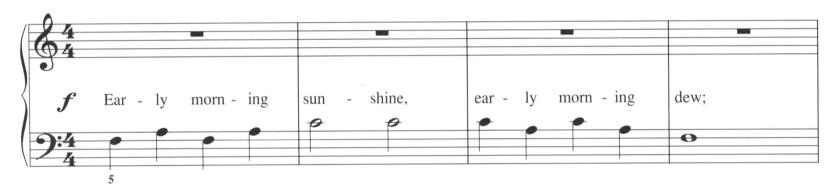

Ear - ly morn - ing   sun - shine,   ear - ly morn - ing   dew;

What a love - ly day, I'll   spend it all with   you.

Teacher

Tempo is the rate of speed at which a piece of music is performed. It is important to play a piece at a tempo that fits its mood and character. You will find a **tempo mark** at the beginning of most pieces.

The Wind and the Breeze

Use the same hand position as you did on page 28.

Slowly

f Hear the au - tumn wind, *p* hear the gen - tle breeze;

f Au - tumn wind, blow hard, breeze, ca - ress the trees. *p*

f Blow, wind, blow! Breeze whis - per low. *p*

See also *The Technic Companion,* p. 12: "Piano-Forte"; and p. 16: "Create moods when you play the piano."

Camping Trip

☆ Circle the 4ths.

Boldly moving

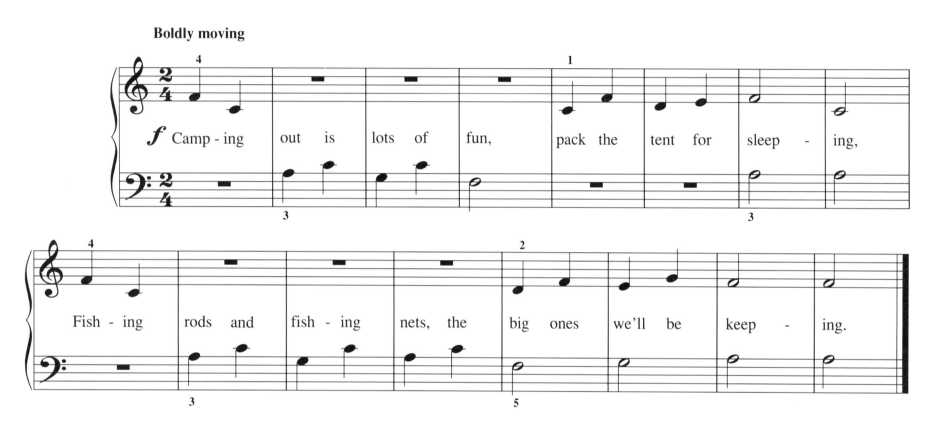

f Camp - ing   out is lots of fun, pack the tent for sleep - ing,

Fish - ing rods and fish - ing nets, the big ones we'll be keep - ing.

☆ Count the beats and clap once for each note in the following exercises:

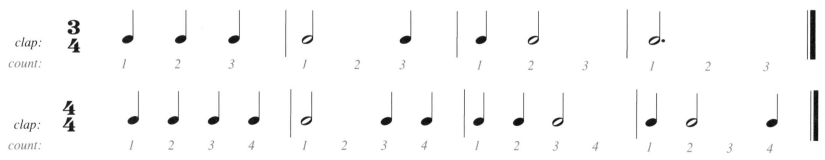

REVIEW

✮ Write the indicated whole notes on the staff below.

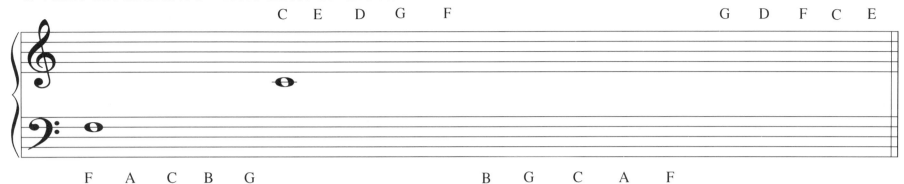

✮ What words do these notes spell out? Write in the letter names.

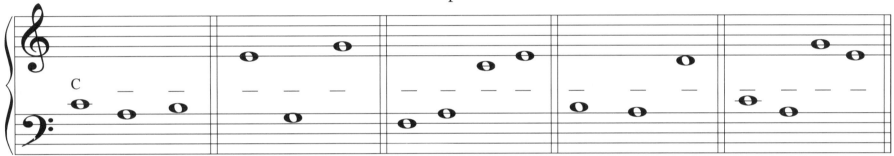

✮ Write in the counts, and put in the missing bar lines.

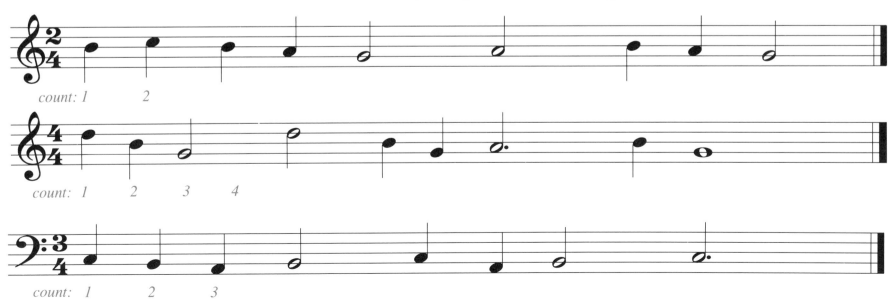

C POSITION

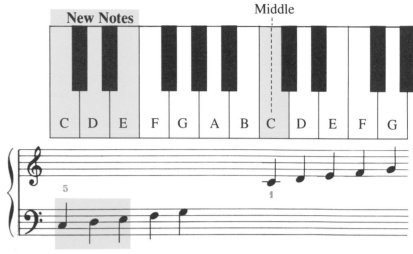

Practice Instructions:

☆ Beginning on C, play
  five-finger pattern.

☆ Clap this rhythm repeatedly:

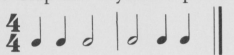

Invitation to a Picnic

☆ Play this piece first with the left hand alone.

Hungarian play tune

Come with me,   sing   with me,   Cook - ies   I'll   bring   with me;

Join   the   fun,   ev - 'ry - one,   Play   in   the   sun   with me!

Teacher

See also *The Technic Companion*, pp. 20, 21.

Round Dance

Use C position (page 36).

> = **accent mark** (stress the note)
mf = *mezzo forte* = medium loud

37

THE SLUR AS LEGATO MARK

The slur is a curved line placed over or under two or more notes.

It indicates the smooth, connected manner of playing called legato.

Legato, an Italian word, means "bound together." The notes bound together by a slur are to be played without any break or gap between the notes; a depressed key is allowed to rise only when the next key is depressed by another finger.

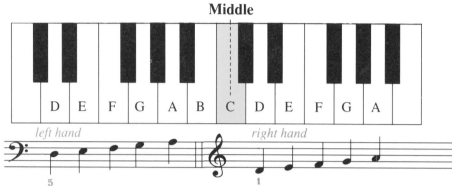

Cloudy Afternoon

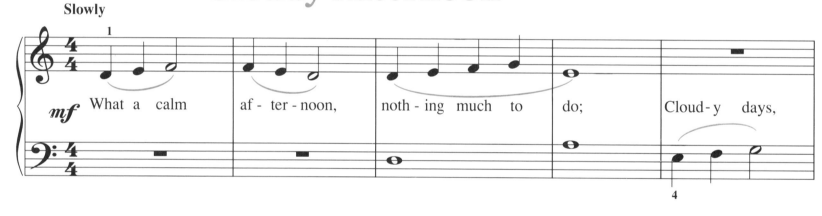

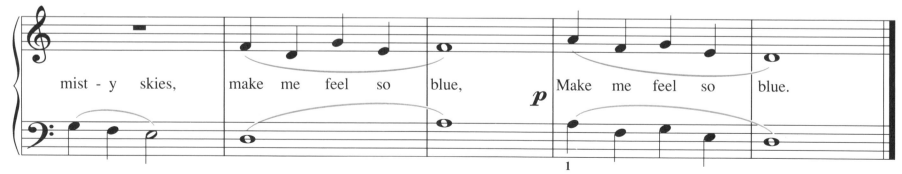

See also *The Technic Companion*, pp. 20, 30, 31.

Jump Tune

Use C position (page 36).

39

Two-Note Slurs

A **two-note slur** has two notes played legato, with a graceful "release" on the second note.

Playing a Two-Note Slur:

1. "Fall" into the first key (from a high wrist to level with forearm) letting the weight of the hand and arm "sink" into the key.
2. Play the second note with legato touch and a graceful rise of the wrist.
3. Continue that motion as the arm and hand follow through, "floating" forward and releasing the key.

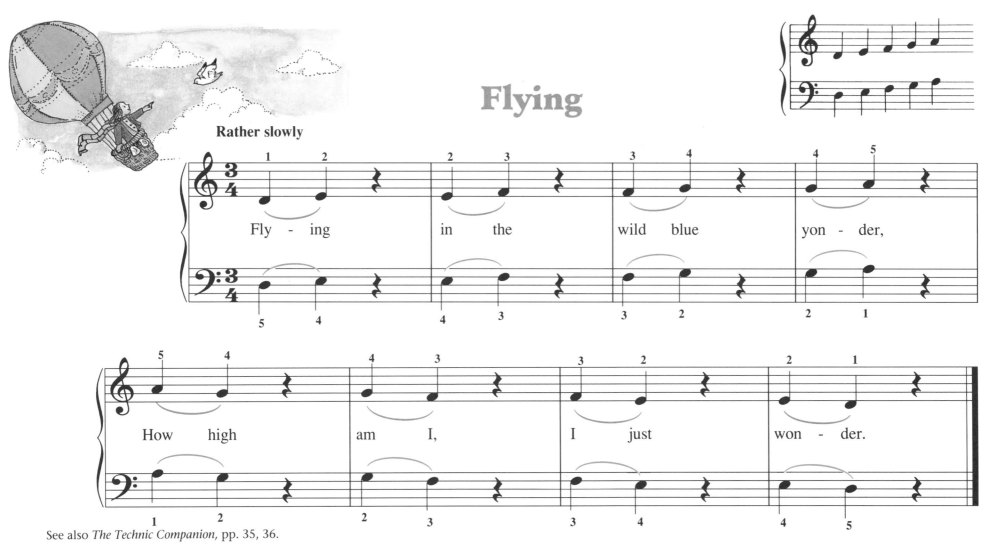

Flying

Rather slowly

Fly - ing   in the   wild blue   yon - der,

How high   am I,   I just   won - der.

See also *The Technic Companion*, pp. 35, 36.

MELODIC AND HARMONIC INTERVALS

Notes played one after another form a melody. The interval between two notes of a melody is called a melodic interval. Name these melodic intervals.

Two or more notes sounded together form harmony. The intervals between two notes sounded together is called a harmonic interval. Name these harmonic intervals:

 This sign, a little bar sitting on the third line, is called a half rest. It indicates silence for two beats (two counts). It has the same time value as a half-note (♩).

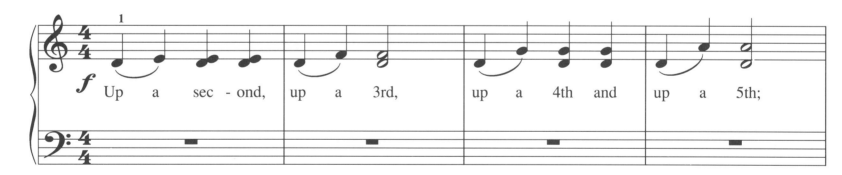

Marching Intervals

Walking tempo

Up a sec - ond, up a 3rd, up a 4th and up a 5th;

Down a sec - ond, down a 3rd, up a 4th, now left, right, stop!

41

THE SLUR AS PHRASE MARK

A group of notes connected by a slur often forms a melody unit called a *phrase*. Phrases are usually two to four measures in length.

Down to the Sea

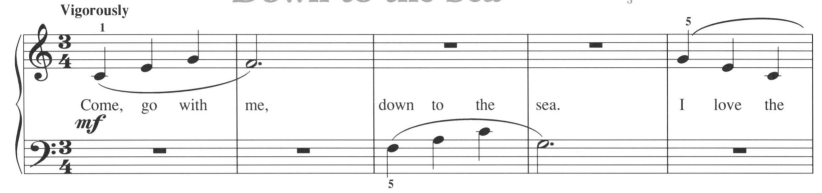

Come, go with me, down to the sea. I love the

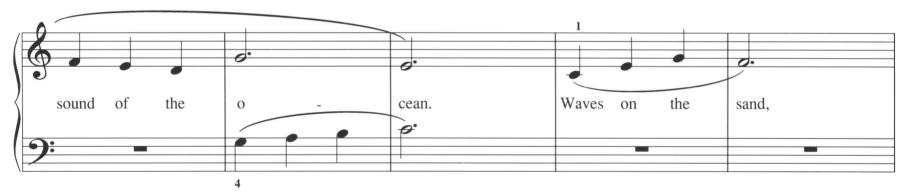

sound of the o - cean. Waves on the sand,

high we will stand, Then we can watch them in mo - tion.

42

THE SHARP SIGN (♯)

Placed in front of a note, the **sharp sign (♯)** *raises* that note to the nearest key to the right, black or white.

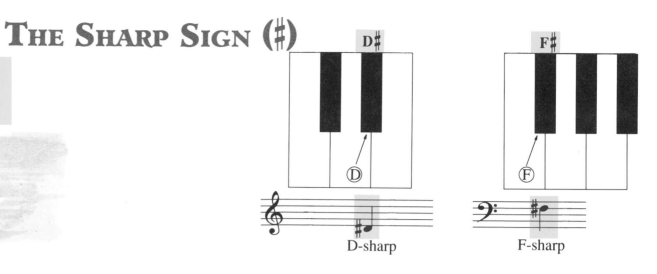

D-sharp

F-sharp

Let's Be Sharp

Use C position (page 36).

Moderately

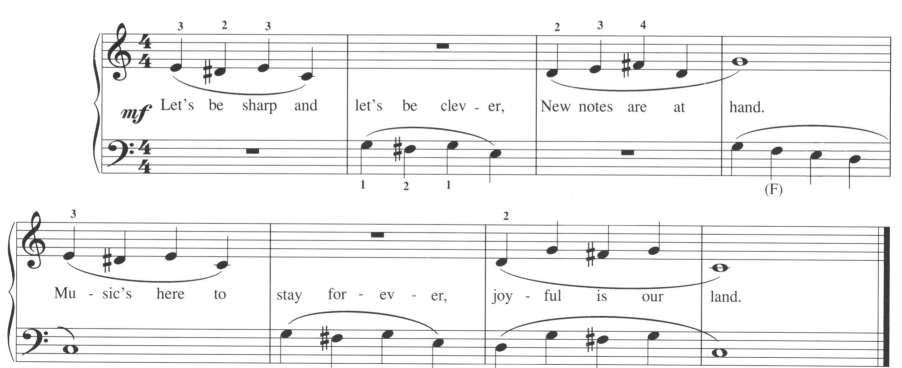

mf Let's be sharp and let's be clev - er, New notes are at hand.

(F)

Mu - sic's here to stay for - ev - er, joy - ful is our land.

All notes in this song are on black keys.

Little Chinese Song

Gently moving

There's a pale moon in the sky, Tem - ple bells are

ring - ing; Let's go walk - ing, you and I, In the

cool of eve - ning, What a love - ly eve - ning.

rit.

Skill Builder: You can also play this piece on all white keys, starting on F.

44

True or False?

_____ 1. This interval is a 4th.

_____ 2. The treble clef is also called the F clef.

_____ 3. This note gets three counts. ♩.

_____ 4. This rest gets two counts. ▬

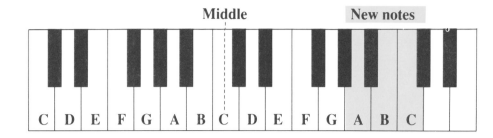

An Alphabet Song

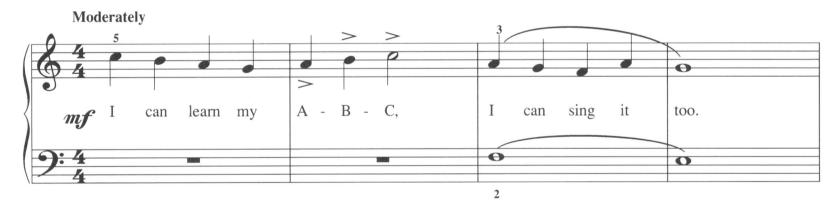

Moderately

mf I can learn my A - B - C, I can sing it too.

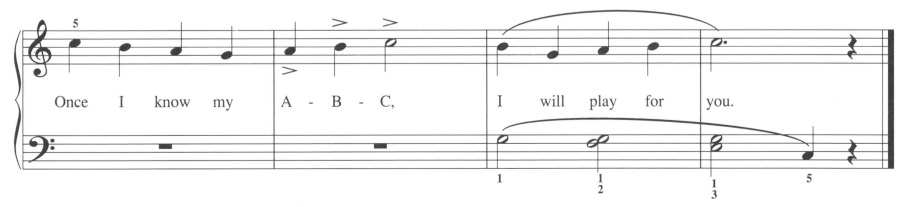

Once I know my A - B - C, I will play for you.

Skating Partners

Smoothly moving

mf Skate hand in hand, through crys - tal land, Skim - ming the edge of our fa - vor - ite pond. Smooth - ly we glide, close, side by side, Watch - ing the sun - set far be - yond.

See also *The Technic Companion,* p. 48.

STACCATO

Staccato is the opposite of legato.

A small dot above or below the notehead (♩̇ ♪̇) indicates that you should play in the short, detached manner called staccato.

After striking the key, the finger bounces back, returning instantly to a raised position.

Play three times

Warm-up

Knock on Wood

Moderately

mf Knock on wood, you'll feel good, You'll have lots of

luck to - day. I would knock wood if I could,

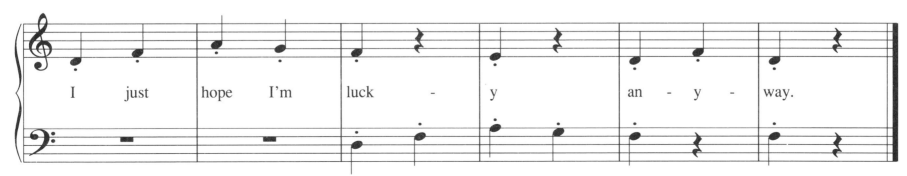

I just hope I'm luck - y an - y - way.

See also *The Technic Companion*, pp. 32–34.

:| The repeat sign tells you to repeat the preceding section.

Cuckoo

☆ Observe the contrast between *staccato* and *legato* touches.

Folk tune

Cuck - oo, cuck - oo, sing night and day.
Cuck - oo, cuck - oo, don't fly a - way.

Nev - er stop sing - ing, joy you are bring - ing, Cuck - oo,

cuck - oo, why can't you stay? Cuck - oo, cuck - oo, cuck - oo.

See also *The Technic Companion,* p. 23: "Third Finger on Black Key"; and pp. 41, 42: "Combining Legato and Staccato Touches."

48

THE FLAT SIGN (♭)

Placed in front of a note, the **flat sign** (♭) **lowers** that note to the nearest key to the left, black or white.

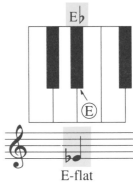

E-flat

A Touch of Blue

Use C position (page 36).

Quite slowly

p Oh, boo - hoo! Think I have the flu.

mf It's a nice day, but I can't play, I'm so blue!

p

EIGHTH-NOTES

♪ This is an **eighth-note**.
It looks like a quarter note with a little flag.

 = one count
Two eighth-notes equal the time value of one quarter-note, one count.

These are two eighth-notes.
Two eighth-notes are connected with a beam instead of being drawn with individual flags.

Count eighth-notes this way:

☆ Clap hands on every note and count aloud.

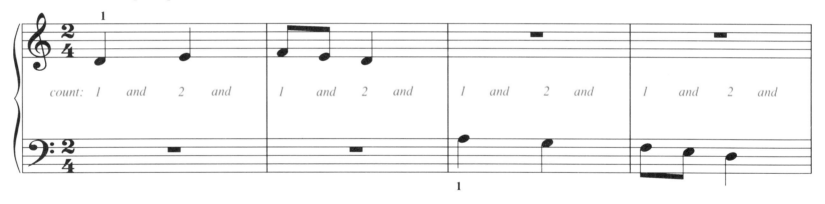

A Brief Stroll

Slow walking tempo

Every time you sing the word "little," you play
two eighth-notes on one beat.

B-flat

Little Indians on Parade

Lively march tempo

f One lit-tle, two lit-tle, three lit-tle In-dians, Four lit-tle, five lit-tle, six lit-tle In-dians,

Sev'n lit-tle, eight lit-tle, nine lit-tle In-dians, Ten lit-tle In-dian boys.

Morning Call

Quite lively

R.H. position same as above.

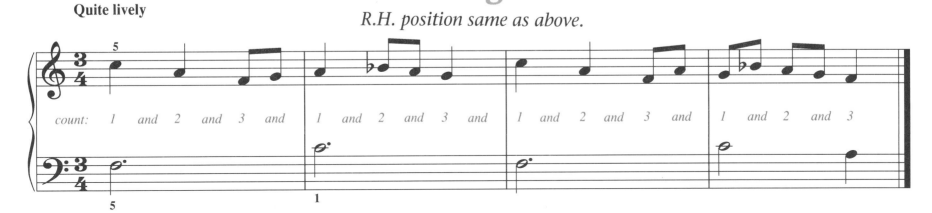

count: 1 and 2 and 3 and   1 and 2 and 3 and   1 and 2 and 3 and   1 and 2 and 3

THE TIE

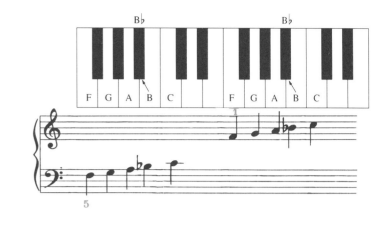

A **tie** is a curved line connecting two neighboring notes that are on the same line or in the same space. When two such notes are tied together we play only the first note and *hold the second note* without striking the key again.

hold it!

Tie

Lullaby for a Rag Doll

☆ Remember the difference between a *slur* (the sign of *legato*) and a *tie*.
☆ Before playing the following piece mark every tie with a **T.**

Slow and gentle rocking motion

Rag doll, rag doll, sweet,_____ Cute from head to feet._____

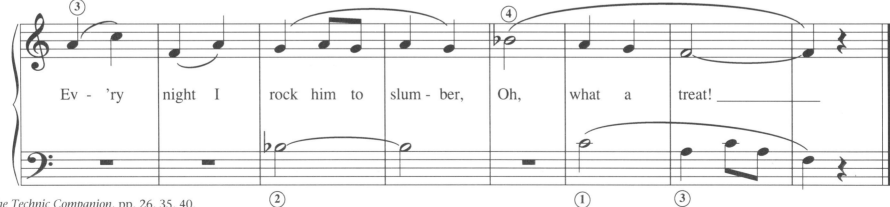

Ev - 'ry night I rock him to slum - ber, Oh, what a treat!_____

See also *The Technic Companion*, pp. 26, 35, 40.

Incomplete Measures

A melody can start on any beat of the measure, not only on the first one.

"Cowboy Song" starts on the last beat of the measure, on count "three."
This note will complete the missing beat in the last measure.

Cowboy Song

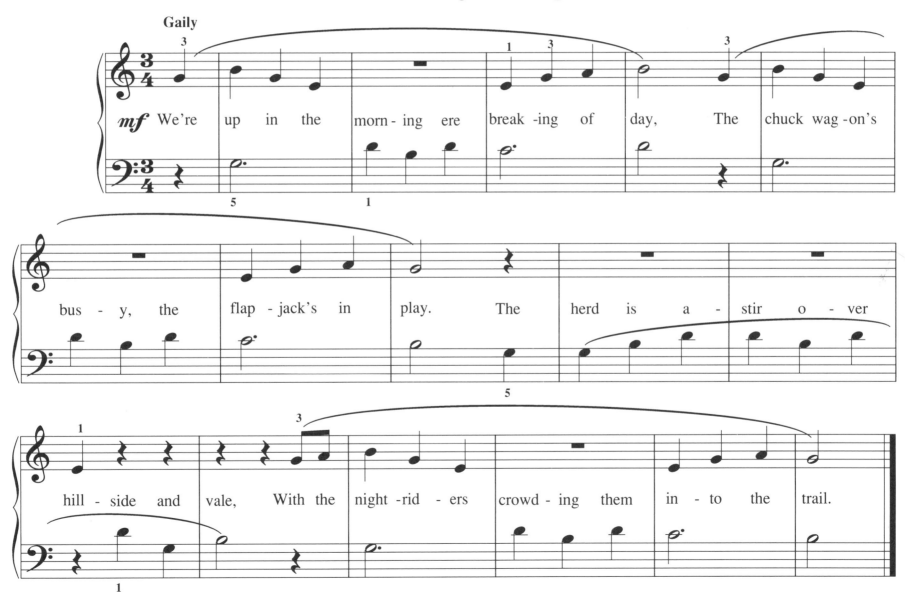

MORE ABOUT SHARPS AND FLATS

Sharps and flats alter not only the note in front of which they stand, but also all other notes
on the same line or in the same space for the rest of that one measure.

✰ Circle those notes which have to be raised or lowered, even though they do not have a sharp or flat in front of them.

Dear Wintertime

See hand position on next page.

Moderately

Folk song

mf Snow fell to - day, Hope it will stay, Then we can sled down the hill,

Ride till we all take a spill, Keep out the sun. Win - ter is fun!

Skill Builder: You may also play this piece with all F's, instead of F♯s. Did you change the mood?

Lightly Row

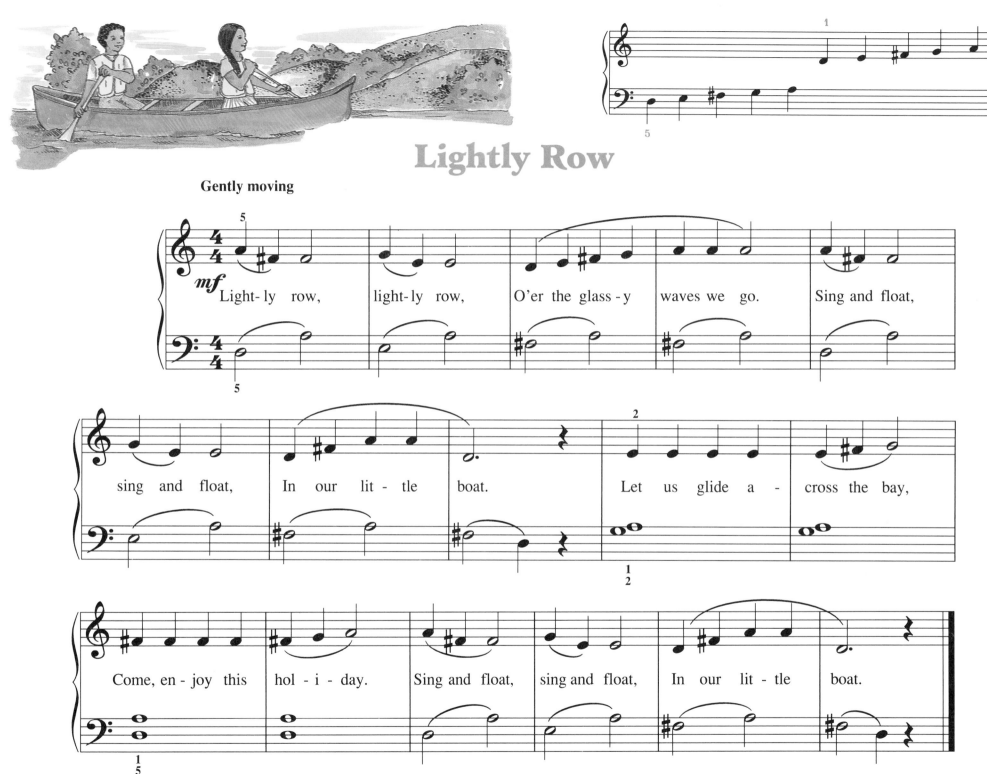

Gently moving

mf

Light-ly row, light-ly row, O'er the glass-y waves we go. Sing and float,

sing and float, In our lit - tle boat. Let us glide a - cross the bay,

Come, en - joy this hol - i - day. Sing and float, sing and float, In our lit - tle boat.

See also *The Technic Companion*, pp. 37, 38.

Warm-up
right hand   *left hand*

No School Today

Moderately slow

I'm in bed, no school to - day, I'm ail - ing I'm a - fraid my
Tucked be - neath my Gran - ny's quilt I'm rest - ing, Ice - cream cones are

health is real - ly fail - ing.
all that I'm re - quest - ing.

(very weakly) Please, bring me two.

★ Write in the letter names of the notes.

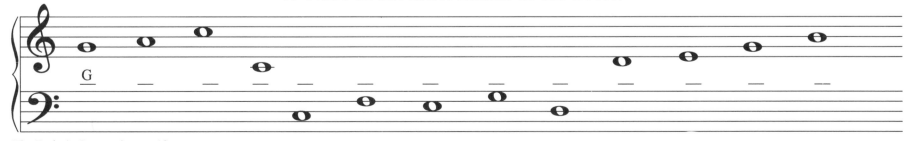

G _ _ _ _ _ _

See also The Technic Companion, *p. 40.*

56

Warm-up

The Ballad of Sad Sam

Moderately

Traditional tunes

Once I loved my   Au - ra Lee,   Chased her night and   day,
Now I love my   Bon - nie lass,   But she sailed a -   way,

Lively

Bring   back,   bring   back, Oh,   bring back my   Bon - nie to   me,   to   me!

Bring   back,   bring   back, Oh,   bring back my   Bon - nie to   me,   to   me!

The Gondolier

Slowly floating

mp Gon - do - lier, your boat is en - chant - ing, Please, good

sir, may I have a ride? Row me down the wa - ters of

Ven - nice, Down ca - nals, a - float on the tide.

rit.

CHORDS

Three notes played together form a chord. There are various types of chords.

☆ Place your right hand on the keyboard in a five-finger position, with the first finger on any white key.
With fingers 1-3-5 strike three keys together (⅗⅛); in doing so you play the simplest type of chord called a triad.

This is how you find the
C chord (for the left hand).

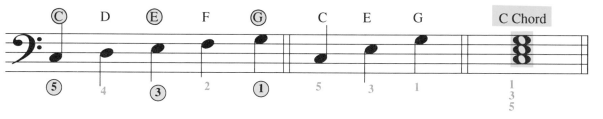

Also play an F chord
and a G chord.

☆ With the right hand play a C chord, an F chord, and a G chord.

Old Woman

Play tune

Skill Builder: Play C, F, and G chords, with each hand, in different octaves.

Sailors' Dance

See also *The Technic Companion*, pp. 59, 60.

60

Warm-up

On the Playground

Play tune (Hungary)

Hop and skip and jump and dip, And 'round and 'round we go! Let us sing

tra - la - la Ding, dong, ding, tra - la- la, You're the king, I'm tra - la - la la, I'm the queen, You're tra - la - la!

61

Warm-up *right hand*

★ Name these intervals.

Valentine Greeting

In a slow, singing manner

mf Do you like me? You are en - tranc - ing, I just

wish that we could go danc - ing. Please don't let me pine,

Tell me you'll be mine. Will you be my sweet Val - en - tine?

See also *The Technic Companion*, p. 51–53: "Balancing Melody and Accompaniment."

True or False?

_____1. Each of these notes is a D:

_____2. Two eighth-notes (♫) have the same time value as one quarter-note (♩).

_____3. A piece always starts on the first beat of a measure.

_____4. Each of these intervals is a third:

_____5. The opposite of *legato* is *staccato*.

_____6. This curved line is a tie:

_____7. This is a quarter rest:

_____8. One of these measures has a beat missing:

Directions of Stems

Notes on or above the middle (third) line have stems pointing down, touching the notehead on the left side.

Notes below the middle (third) line have stems pointing up, touching the notehead on the right side.

Draw stems for the following notes.

The **natural sign** (♮) cancels a sharp or a flat. When you see the sign in front of a note, you play the original white key.

Tricks in Black and White

Autumn Is Coming

Au - tumn is com - ing, clear and cold.
Leaves will be fall - ing, red and gold.

Wind sends them fly - ing,

see them take wing, But they'll grow back and be green in the spring.

See also *The Technic Companion*, p. 49.

64

Changing Hand Positions

Raindrops on the Windowpane

Playfully moving

mf

Tip - toe through the | gar - den in a | show — er. | | Care-ful now, don't

③ *new hand-position for right hand*

step up - on a | flow — er. | | *f* Then we'll hear the | rain | *p* on the win-dow

pane; | *mf* Pat - ter, pit - ter, | pat - ter, what a | nice re - | frain.

See also *The Technic Companion*, pp. 32–34.

Song of Brotherhood

See also *The Technic Companion*, p. 60.

The Hurdy-Gurdy Man

See also *The Technic Companion*, pp. 51, 52; and p. 60.

The right pedal of the piano, when depressed, sustains the sound. Depress the pedal silently with the ball of your right foot. (The heel stays on the floor.)

PEDAL

Pedal sign:
press   lift

Recital Waltz

Play this measure the first time   *Play this measure the second time*

1.   2.

See also *The Technic Companion*, pp. 54, 55.

Junior Boogie

Moderately, with a strong beat

crescendo or *cresc.* (kre-shen-do) = **gradually louder**

diminuendo or *dim.* (de-me-noo-en-do) = **gradually softer**

At a Gypsy Campfire

See also *The Technic Companion,* pp. 12, 61.

Hand Positions:

Warm-up

Zulu War Chant

Vigorous jungle beat

Fine (end)

f Aye - ze - ka zoom-ba, zoom-ba, zoom-ba, Aye - ze - ka zoom-ba, zoom -ba - ay,

Hail   the   Zu - lu   war-ri-or!   Hail   the   Zu - lu   chief!

Repeat from start to Fine
(with repetition)

See also *The Technic Companion,* pp. 18, 19.

GLOSSARY

accent mark: > stress the note

bar lines: vertical lines dividing the staff into *measures*

bass clef: 𝄢 indicates lower notes on the staff, usually played by the left hand

chord: three tones played together

crescendo (*cresc.*): gradually louder

diminuendo (*dim.*): gradually softer

dotted half-note: 𝅗𝅥. (three counts)

double bar line: indicates the end of a piece

eighth-note: ♪ (one half count)

f: *forte*—loud

F clef: another name for the *bass clef*

Fine *(fee-nay):* the end

flat: ♭ lowers the note by a *half-step*

forte: loud

G clef: another name for the *treble clef*

grand staff: a treble staff and a bass staff connected by a vertical line and a brace (bracket)

half-step: the distance between one key and the very next key, black or white

half-note: 𝅗𝅥 (two counts)

interval: the distance between two tones

legato: smooth, connected manner of playing; marked by a *slur*

letter names of the keys A B C D E F G (the musical alphabet)

measure: the segment of music between two *bar lines* on the staff

mf: *mezzo forte*—medium loud

Middle C: the white key just to the left of the two black keys in the middle of the keyboard

mp: *mezzo piano*—medium soft

natural: ♮ cancels a *sharp* or a *flat*

note: a written symbol representing a tone

note value: the duration or length of a *note*

octave: the interval of eight notes (both notes of the interval have the same letter-name)

p: *piano*—soft

pedal: part of the piano mechanism which, when depressed by the right foot, sustains the sound

phrase: a melody unit, usually two to four measures in length

piano: soft

quarter-note: ♩ (one count)

repeat sign: :‖ means repeat the preceding section

rest signs: 𝄽 = quarter-rest, ‒ = half-rest, ‑ = whole-rest

rhythm: the sound pattern formed by a group of tones and pauses of various lengths

ritardando (*rit.*): gradually slower

sharp: ♯ raises the note by a *half-step*

skip: when notes skip from a line to the next line, or from a space to the next space

slur: a curved line over or under a note group, indicating *legato*

staccato (*stacc.*): a detached manner of playing, indicated by a dot over or under the note

step: when notes move stepwise from a space to the next line or from a line to the next space

tempo: the rate of speed in music

tie: a curved line connecting two neighboring notes on the same line or in the same space

time signature: two numbers written at the beginning of a piece, indicating the number of beats in a *measure* and the type of *note* that gets one count

treble clef: 𝄞 indicates higher notes, usually played by the right hand

triad: a *chord* consisting of three tones; the root (lowest tone), with the intervals of the third and the fifth

whole-note: ○ (four counts)